When the Door Closes...

Do Something Amazing!

A Journey of Trust and Obedience ...

JACQUELINE D. JENKINS, ED.D.

Illustrated by Bryon Tann

ISBN 978-1-0980-3204-3 (paperback)
ISBN 978-1-0980-3205-0 (digital)

Christian Faith Publishing, Inc.
832 Park Avenue
Meadville, PA 16335
www.christianfaithpublishing.com

Printed in the United States of America

Dedication

I dedicate this labor of love back to God.
He is the source of my inspiration.

"When one door closes another door opens;
But we so often look so long and so
regretfully upon the closed door,
That we do not see the ones which opens for us."
—Alexander Graham Bell

Contents

Foreword

I am honored to write this foreword. For not only is
Dr. Jenkins a mentor, spiritual advisor and vessel
That has been chosen to convey the power of faith and devotion…
She is also my mother.
Dr. Jenkins always encourages me and been very instrumental
In the strengthening of my relationship with God.
This book is not just about the power of prayer and faith.
It speaks to the life experiences, obstacles, and decisions
many are faced with daily.
Distractions are at times disguised as
desirable outcomes to situations,
Only to deter you from your true level of elevation.
This book gives an account of trusting
God's process and understanding
That there is purpose in your pain.
My mother gave me a quote that I live by everyday:
"God has not elevated you to this current
level in your life to desert you now."
Stop waiting for that light at the end of
the tunnel and light it yourself.
Be patient and remain forever faithful…
Enjoy your journey my friend.

—Alexis V. Cleveland

Introduction

A closed door can be a devastating experience. Perhaps we have lost a job or a loved one. Other times, it is a treasured opportunity, a hope, or a dream that seemed to vanish right before our very eyes. In some instances, the loss feels crippling—whatever or whomever is no longer here, because the door has closed. However, losing something at some point is inevitable. The key is how we handle the experience. Think for a moment, about the past doors that have closed in your life. I certainly have had my share of closed-door experiences. Actually, if you asked me, like a lot of you I have had more than my fair share of closed-door experiences. By the way, does anyone know what the fair share is, because I'm sure mine is multiplied by a few. When we experience loss, no matter what the loss is, we go through a season of void, which triggers human emotion. The greater the loss, the stronger and deeper the feelings. How do you manage the disappointment? Sometimes we need help to get through these times. I am grateful that I have God as my help. I'm curious, what or who is your help? Where do you turn for support?

Well, when you trust God no matter what the circumstance, the tough times become more bearable. Of course, God did not guarantee that all our days would be sunny. However, He did remind us that through the storms, "God is faithful, and he will not let you be tempted beyond your ability, but with the temptation he will also provide the way of escape, that you may be able to endure it" (1 Corinthians 19:13 ESV). Also, if you believe that He supplies all of our needs, then you have to believe that He will give us the strength we need for the journey. I'm thankful for my struggles, because without them, I would have never stumbled upon my strength. Let's talk about the closed-door experience.

"SEEK His will IN All you do,
AND HE will show you which
Path to TAKE" PROVERbs 3:6

Chapter One

Seeking God

The Letter

Our term is coming to a close. What a roller-coaster ride. Reality is setting in as the race is over and we lost. Door slammed shut! *Boom!* I've never been on a losing team. However, I have experienced losing situations. At least that's how they all felt to me at the time. I've not had a real opportunity to process what was happening because it has only been a few weeks, and it was my favorite time of year—the Christmas holidays. Not an accident, I'm sure. God knows I love how the atmosphere feels this time of year. As people, we transform into a season of givers. Our attitudes are different, and we show genuine care and concern for our fellow man. Regardless of how you feel about the holiday season, or why it's recognized, or how it's celebrated, you can't deny the incredible feelings we share this time of year. Somehow life always seems to be all right, especially if you are not pressured into the traditions of the holiday. During this season, I am excited to celebrate the birth of Jesus, and for me, it's pointless to debate when or where he was born. What matters is that he was born.

This mid-December morning, the office was buzzing with conversation about the upcoming holidays. Despite the circumstances, the holiday season had me feeling pretty amazing. As my colleague and I were talking in my office, envelopes were handed to each of us. We briefly looked at each other with the "did that just happen?" look. Of course, on that cold December day, we both knew what was inside the envelopes without even opening them since neither of us had been asked to meet to discuss our future. Sure enough, mine was a letter thanking me for my service and advising me that my position was either being eliminated or being filled by someone else. At this point, my colleague had already understandably exited my office, and I sat there slightly disappointed. Even though I had not had a meeting, I simply did not think my assignment was done. I also knew that my work related to advancing our role in the activities connected to ensuring quality education for all children was significant, especially children living in the city. I was also told repeatedly by people, other than God, not to worry because I would be fine.

As I processed what had just occurred, in my head I heard the beginning of the song "Thriller" by Michael Jackson, the king of pop. You know the one where the door is creaking, and that wicked laughter gets louder as the door slams shut! I heard that hysterical laughter ringing in my head, and with shock in my heart for some odd reason, I felt like that creaking sound was the door closing on a long and successful professional career—or so I thought....

The Unknown

In that moment, I thought, *Unemployed, what is that?* I have been blessed in that I have always been employed. I've had a job since my career began after college, with no breaks in my service. *What is this, and, God, where are you?* As I tried to collect myself and my thoughts (after all, I was sitting in my office at work), the first thing I thought about was the fact that I knew that I had heard God very clearly just four years earlier telling me to leave my secure dream job to take this job. Clearly this job is now a temporary one, ending after four years. Listening to hear from God is an intimate process. As with our natural relationships, we don't always hear from God when we want to hear from him. You know, "He may not come when you want Him but He's always right on time." Of course, my pressing question is, What are we doing here? I really needed to hear from God.

Hearing God requires that we earnestly seek to develop a genuine relationship with Him. Typically, we do not usually hold long, deep conversations with strangers. When we really need to talk with someone, we usually reach out to the individuals we know and have a trusting relationship. Maybe that's just me. That conversation is always a dialogue between two people. One person talking, one person listening—repeat. God desires that same intimacy with us. I believe if we really want to hear God, we have to work hard at getting to know Him. Whenever we call, He will always answer. So how do we do that, I heard someone ask. That's the right question too: How do we get to know God? The same way we get to know someone that we've met and want to know better. We spend time with them. Simply seek God because He is looking for you. "The Lord looks down from heaven on all mankind to see if there are any who understand, any who seek God" (Psalm 14:2 NIV). However, once we begin to hear God, we also become accountable **to** God. Just like school, we can't be held accountable for what we don't know. However, once we have been taught and tested, we are now responsible for the knowledge. That makes sense—right? Today as I talk to God, I need Him to talk to me. I am waiting to hear from Him. Waiting is hard; it's a lesson and a book in itself—"Waiting on God."

Are you waiting for an answer because the door has closed? Did the door close on a relationship that has ended? Perhaps you are waiting because you have prayed for a specific answer to a certain prayer. Maybe you are dealing with a situation that has you feeling like you are down to what you believe is the last straw, and you just learned the door closed because the answer is no to "your" last hope. What's the saying, "When you believe you are down to nothing, God is always up to something." Under those circumstances, you should expect God to show up—I do! Guess what? He always does too!

My Work

Where am I now? I thought I had previously found the perfect job for me before this one. I had been working in my craft (more than twenty years), and I worked for an organization that was making a difference in the lives of others. The best of both worlds. My job included a six-figure salary, great benefits, and the best administrative team ever! I thought I would retire from that place. After all, I worked hard to prepare myself. Hard work and preparation meeting opportunity—isn't that supposed to be the definition of success? What's funny about that is, just when I thought I had my plan all figured out, here comes God with His plan. You know what they say, "If you want to make God laugh, tell Him your plan."

I briefly started to think about the other employment opportunities that I turned down recently because God said no for one reason or another. Did you get that? They said yes, and God said no! I thought they were great opportunities too, and some were places I had not submitted applications. Someone once told me that when you do really great work, you should never have to "apply" for employment. Offers should come to you. Were they right? Today my question is, Why was me leaving such a great job to take this temporary job so important to God? As my head began to spin, I started to think about the scariness of the unknown that had caught me slightly off guard. For some strange reason, this door not only feels like it closed, it feels like it's slammed shut! I briefly started entertaining the foolishness of whose fault this was and how I found myself in such a mess. (Now that's another book—***"Conversations with God.")***

I was beginning to feel like I was sitting in a small boat in the middle of a major storm. Thankfully, that feeling was brief. After only a few moments of sitting in a fog, and before I could even begin to think about stressing over this, a small, still voice asked, "Who can speak and have it happen if the Lord has not decreed it?" (Lamentations 3:37, NIV). I continued to sit quietly as I thought about that question, and suddenly a sense of peace came over me. I felt like my daddy had just given me the biggest hug and told me everything was okay. At that very moment I felt safe. I don't know about you, but there is nothing like daddy's hug.

The Clarity

It seemed like the headlights came on and the seas calmed. The fog started to dissipate, and the sun began to shine brightly on that cold December day. Suddenly, while I had no idea what was next, I was comforted knowing that God was already ahead of the situation and I could trust Him; I had to trust Him. What choice did I have? I could breathe knowing with great confidence that God was still in charge and He was in complete control. Clearly, unemployment could not be God's final answer. I have responsibilities and bills, so I need resources to support them. Also, I must have access to God's resources to be able to be a blessing and continue to do His work. So there had to be a plan, and I was comforted knowing that I was not alone.

After all, God said, "Do not be anxious about anything, but in every situation, by prayer and petition, with thanksgiving, present your requests to God. And the peace of God, which transcends all understanding, will guard your hearts and your minds in Christ Jesus" (Philippians 4:6–7 NIV). Right then because I know God, I knew peace. I already knew what requests I planned to put before God as my thinking briefly shifted as I thought about my other colleagues. I could not imagine any of them facing similar uncertainty without having a relationship with God. I immediately began to pray for them.

This could have been the making of a catastrophic day. On the outside, my life looked like it had just been turned upside down. Instead, I was at peace because I knew I had faith in God. My faith in God allowed me to trust Him. That trust gave me peace. Not just regular peace, but the peace that flows like a river. It was the kind of peace that surpasses all understanding. I had the peace of God. Have you experienced the true peace of God? Think about that for a moment. What does God's peace mean to you? If God is, the God of Peace (1 Thessalonians 5:23 NIV), then to know God is to know His peace. "Peace I leave with you, my peace I give to you; not as the world gives do I give to you" (John 14:27 NKJV). When we make the Lord our refuge, then we are able to dwell in the peace of God. Where do you live?

The Assignment

God's peacefulness allowed me to think about my tomorrows without anxiety. As I thought about my letter, I understood that God had allowed the action based on His earlier question. That also had to mean that He had an amazing plan for me, and that excited me. This was the end of the chapter and not the end of the story. It couldn't be the end of the story. There had to be more. What was next? I asked God, What are you doing now? The unknown was scary and exciting at the same time! Imagine that! I heard you again… How did I come to that conclusion? Thank you for asking. Let's go back a bit. Just four years earlier, God asked me to accept a job offer, and I said yes. This was a job I certainly would have never thought about applying for, because taking the job made no sense either. The position was an appointed position, and that meant four years of security. Remember I told you, I had a great job, in a great place, doing great things. God, are you really asking me to walk away?

However, out of sheer and utter obedience to God, I took a deep breath and said yes! That "yes" and the many yesses that followed ultimately caused me to now be unemployed. Right now, moving with God feels like a great sacrifice for me. Of course, God already knew this would be the case. So I know my blessing is going to be mind-boggling because I know there just had to be more of God's story to be told. This isn't even a good ending. Besides, if this was the end of the story, where is God's glory in this experience? I'm supposed to be his representative. My life is supposed to be an example of what following God looks like and feels like so others will want to "taste and see that the Lord is good; blessed is the one who takes refuge in him" (Psalm 34:8 NIV). This door has slammed shut, so it must be time for God to do something amazing!

God has reminded me countless times before that nothing happens to me without his permission. Based on His earlier question, today was no exception. My steps are ordered by God, and sometimes my steps take me to places that do not immediately include me but are ultimately about me. Hmmm…think about that for a moment. Apparently, this assignment was no different. I was sent to do God's work. So, initially this move was about others, but ultimately this will be about me. And here we are…a familiar place. I have previously found myself on assignment in places and situations that were initially about other people and their circumstances, and I was simply the conduit.

The Conduit

A conduit is the vessel or vehicle by which things move from one place to another. The *KJV Dictionary* defines conduit as "a canal or pipe for the conveyance of water. Conduits are made of [strong materials such as] lead, stone, cast iron, wood, etc. [A conduit is] a vessel that conveys the blood or other fluid." Apparently, the conduit is a necessary mechanism.

The conduit is created by a manufacturer, but it's the builder who sets it in place and tests it for structural integrity against leaks and the like. If the conduit works properly, then it's put into place to perform its purpose. However, what's interesting is, no matter how important the conduit is to the manufacturer, it has no ability to determine when, where, or how it will be used. The builder determines when the conduit will be used to fulfill its purpose—to transfer something from its source to its intended destination. It's like activation! Did you get that? You're about to bake a cake and you have all of the ingredients that you need. However, if you don't do something with those ingredients, then you will never have a cake. God gives us everything we need when we are born. We are required to connect the dots in order to see the full picture.

Okay, how about this: think about electricity and the fact that regardless of how powerful electricity is, alone it cannot get from one point to another without a channel—the conduit. The conduit is the mechanism that allows the electricity to flow. It's the thing that forces movement. No matter how important electricity is, it is powerless without a conduit to travel.

Now, why are we talking about conduits? I love your questions. Just like natural conduits, I believe people are also conduits, for Christ. I believe conduits are everywhere. Not only is God the source of what passes through the conduit spiritually, He also decides when it is time to activate a conduit. Imagine, something in your life is interfering with God's purpose (free will?). God may send a conduit to be the vehicle He uses to move or cause redirection of something, therefore creating a pathway for Him to move. However, what is not always clear is, we may or may not be aware of what has to be moved, which makes for a very interesting experience.

Conduits are pretty special to God. Being ready to move on God's behalf is an awesome responsibility. Preparedness is the key. When the conduit is neglected, it loses its ability to fully achieve its purpose. If the conduit becomes clogged or restricted, that interferes with the flow of God. The passageway must be reopened. If the conduit is left unchecked, it could over time simply become useless. Conduits play a very important role.

Think about an instance when someone came into your life and affected great change. The change was so profound that you can immediately recall the name(s) of those individuals. This was change you knew you needed, and you welcomed the change. Maybe not right away, I heard you. Perhaps it was change you knew you needed but weren't so excited about in the beginning. The third possibility is, it was change you knew nothing about! Now talk about interesting. You, my friend, were entertaining a conduit!

Through interaction, you eventually discovered that something had to move and move soon. Maybe it was you who needed to move. The conduit furthers God's purpose, and with God's help causes something or someone to move. This is why conduits must work diligently to ensure their vessels are free-flowing in order to receive and transmit on God's behalf.

Being a conduit is not only a blessing to the individual, it is also an opportunity to be a blessing in ministry. I believe conduits for God are full of His love. I don't think it is possible to disrupt someone's life the way a conduit can, without sprinkles of God's love along the way. Even Mary Poppins said, "a spoonful of sugar helps the medicine go down."

The Work

People recognize conduits by the joy and fullness of God they feel when they come into their presence. Now I agree, people will describe that feeling in many different ways. I cannot tell you the countless times I have had people in my office looking for something, or nothing at all. Some days they were there for answers or guidance. Other days someone might simply need encouragement. A good old dose of God's love and tender kindness through a smile or good conversation to get through the day. I know I was sent to this place to be a conduit. Many things happened to and through people while we were here. Much had to be done. We were sent to fulfill many purposes. God's plan affected many lives during our stay, regardless of the brevity.

Being used by God as a conduit is an honor and a great privilege that also includes great responsibility. Even though the assignment may include moments of discomfort and difficulty, knowing that you have been chosen by God to complete an assignment should provide confidence and bring the individual extraordinary joy and peace. You know, it's one thing when you choose God; however, it's something extra special when God choses you. In John 15:16 NIV, Jesus says, "You did not choose me, but I chose you and appointed you so that you might go and bear fruit—fruit that will last—and so that whatever you ask in my name the Father will give you."

Someone is feeling burdened right now because of the magnitude of the task God has called you to do. Whatever is being asked of you, embrace the opportunity to show God your faithfulness, so He can show you His faithfulness. He's waiting for you. If you take one step, He will take two. Please don't miss the opportunity to position yourself to receive all God has for you.

The Plan

Witnessing God's plan unfold is like watching a good movie. When we willingly allow ourselves to be used by God, the joy and the peace of God becomes evident. This is the peace and joy that people need to see especially when it otherwise looks dark. I believe being used by God means more than simply being influenced by God. I think it means God becomes part of the fiber of who we are as individual believers.

Seeking, learning, knowing more about God is a lifelong process. What's great about that is, it comes with many mutual benefits.

I have found that when we seek God, not only do we learn more about Him, we also learn more about ourselves and our own purpose. When we reach a crossroad, such as the one I am currently experiencing, knowing God encourages us not to turn away from Him. This is the time to turn to God and seek Him more than ever for stability, especially if it feels like a hurricane is swirling. Feeling sick is okay; however, knowing where to find the medication is what's important. If we were feeling extremely ill, we wouldn't go to an amusement park to feel better. We would go to the doctor or hospital—right?

What's interesting, though, is, God seems to use us most when we are at our greatest need. He always seems to know how to meet my needs. What's funny about that is that it usually happens when He allows me to minister to the needs of someone else. Being used by God to minister to the needs of others has a way of providing personal comfort, because that's where our comfort comes from—within. He "who comforts us in all our troubles, so that we can comfort those in any trouble with the comfort we ourselves receive from God" (2 Corinthians 1:3–4 NIV). A lot happens on the inside. Do you notice that?

When we accept the honor of being used by God, we are keenly aware of God working in and through us. We learn to trust Him more and understand that regardless of what we see with our natural eye, He has everything under control and is working it out. I believe that seeking God with an open heart causes His genuine love and endless peacefulness to ooze from the believer, and it's contagious. It is our responsibility to represent God in such a way that people want what they see and want even more of how that makes them feel.

When we keep our eyes stayed on the prize, we won't allow situations to derail us so quickly. Wherever we go, God goes too.

"I love those who love Me, and those who seek me diligently and find me."
Proverbs 8:17

There is power in the journey…

To do extraordinary things…

Chapter Two

Being Used by God

God's Electricity—The Change Agent

Have you ever been used by God? Can you say with great confidence that you have ever had the pleasure of being truly used by God? I mean, do you believe that you have been specifically chosen to further God's plan in someone's life? Has God ever asked you to do something that made no sense to you? Something like walk away from a wonderful, secure job to take a job with no security? What about being asked to deliver a personalized message to someone you barely know, or don't know at all, simply because God asked you to share a word? Have you ever been told that when you walk into a room, "the atmosphere changes"?

More questions. What about humiliation? Have you suffered public humiliation for God's sake by keeping silent when you are asked not to respond to the negative situation, even when you're completely innocent? You know—hold your peace and let the Lord fight your battle. We sing about being victorious when that happens because "the LORD will fight for you; you need only to be still" (Exodus 14:14 NIV). Each of the questions I have asked you represents a scenario in my life when I was being used by God to "do something" or "say something."

Some instances required a personal sacrifice on my part. I was the conduit God chose to fulfill His specific purpose for someone else. Writing this book and being so personal is a perfect example of being used by God and my obedience. He asked me to document my "closed-door" experience in an effort to encourage and be a blessing to someone else. Why, you ask, would I be so willing to make such significant sacrifices repeatedly for God? Simply because He asked—it's a choice. It's like listening to your parents, and besides, God said,

"If you love me, you will obey what I command" (John 14:15 NIRV). Some things in our lives are easier to surrender or control than others.

Since we do not know God's plan, we really have no idea what our actions mean. We don't know the reason, nor do we always understand the impact. We also do not know what failing to act means. Most of all, when we don't act, I believe we miss an opportunity to not only be a blessing, but we also miss an opportunity to please God. Can you imagine if Mary and Joseph said no to God? That was a lot to ask—right?

I can recall a time when I was stripped of my responsibilities in a very public way, and for no good reason that I could identify. In circumstances like that, finding the peace to quiet the desire to publicly fight back takes obedience and trust as you wait for vindication. You can only accomplish that by spending time getting to know God and learning how to love God even when you are being tested.

I knew that situation was also God, and somehow, I would be vindicated. However, in the meantime, God said for me to fix my face and act like I knew it was Him. That meant for me not to make it about anything or anyone, even though I was frustrated beyond words. When God repeatedly says He will take care of you and does so over and over again, you learn to believe Him. **Being a conduit for God also means being willing to be a change agent.**

As usual, that experience turned out to be divine protection and one big blessing. We will chat about that another time. That's why it's so important to simply trust God. Even when it looks bleak. Besides, God said, "I have given you authority to trample on snakes and scorpions and to overcome all the power of the enemy; nothing will harm you. However, do not rejoice that the spirits submit to you, but rejoice that your names are written in heaven" (Luke 10:19–20, NIV). Anyway, He's always right—that's why I trust Him.

Prayers and Blessings

I can think of another time when I prayed for a specific blessing. When God answered and I received the blessing, I was so excited. However, what I didn't realize then was that when God does something great for us—He is looking for us to do something great for Him too. Pay it forward! He never blesses us to keep the blessing to ourselves. He blesses us so we can be a blessing to others. My mom would say, God can't bless a closed fist. Are you selfish with your blessings? Have you been wondering why you have been receiving fewer blessings? Sharing is caring...at least that's what my grandson tells me.

This particular blessing was a new job in an office that I had visited countless times before. Just prior to my first day, I happened to run into an employee who was leaving the department. The individual—a pastor—told me that when he asked God who was his replacement in the department, God told him it was me. I didn't really understand that conversation at the time because I was not hired to fill his specific position. A few weeks later, I arrived at work as an employee of the department. On that day, I felt like I had walked into the lion's den. While the lights were on in the office, it felt cold and dark. I immediately asked God, *What is this and why am I here?* I didn't know much, but I knew it was time to pray. I knew these were not going to be ordinary prayers. I felt like I had walked into a battle zone. That experience kept me on my knees because it was so painful at times. Of course, that was the plan to draw me closer to God. I had been sent to cultivate the seeds of the previous worker (God's disciple). I was in battle on God's behalf, and I was the seed protector. That's why it's so important to know your role in God's plan. I learned so much about me and God, my prayer life, my spiritual gifts, and my ministry as an intercessor. I was the spiritual replacement. I first had to learn what that meant. Then I had to figure out how to be the spiritual replacement. Many of the individuals I met during that experience over thirty years ago, I am still connected to today. I told you, it was amazing to watch God work. I now understand the role of a spiritual replacement, watching over the flock.

While I knew I was there to learn about being a spiritual replacement, there were many other things I needed to learn about too (like spiritual warfare). God had to teach me how to fight without using my fists. Now that was tough since I grew up in the inner city. God needs fighters though to complete His work, and somebody has to get the tough assignments and the dirty jobs. His assignments are not always for the faint of heart. In addition to my tasks, I was also charged with developing and cultivating new relationships. During that class, a lot of those lessons took me over three years to figure out. Learning how to help people by meeting them right where they are without judgment was one of my lessons. Sometimes, in order to lead them out of darkness, you have to be willing to go to the darkness. That assignment was no picnic for me, and it had many layers of teaching. The assignment was tough because it was OJT (on-the-job training). Some things I knew and other things I had to figure out along the way. Pray without ceasing was the message. Ironically, that was the preached message when I received Christ as my Savior a long time ago. You also can't be an intercessor without constant prayer. However, after a while I was feeling like I was at my wits' end. While I felt like I was doing really good work for God, the attacks kept coming. They were coming so frequently I couldn't see the progress. I didn't feel like I knew what I was doing. All I knew to do was to pray, and pray, and pray some more. I later learned that was the focus of the assignment.

I am reminded of a particularly difficult situation that immediately impacted several employees through no fault of their own. At the ninth hour, my task was to meet with these employees. People had no idea they were about to lose their jobs. I was sick to my stomach. I didn't sleep the night before. God, how in the world do I deliver such unfortunate news to these people? I lay in God's presence for strength, for wisdom, and for compassion. Most important, I asked that God's will be done. Those employee meetings turned out to be some of the most amazing memories I have of my career. While those individuals were angry and upset, I challenged those employees to think outside the box and to embrace change. I knew some of their circumstances, and while I knew a door was closing, I also saw God opening new doors. I began to minister to them. Even though I didn't know what their respective beliefs were, we had church in my office that day over and over again. I learned so much about God and my relationship with him during that experience. I watched Him literally and repeatedly turn earthquakes into mild tremors, right before my very eyes. That was a great day. I was sold out!

Each day, just before work started, I had daily work devotions for strength. Now, I knew why I was there, and I was thankful for that wonderful experience. While that was my success story, that was a long assignment in a difficult work environment. Even after that great experience, I kept hearing, "Don't celebrate too quickly, they're coming back." Through the continued difficulty, one morning I remember crying out to God, saying this assignment was too hard for me. God answered, telling me to look around. As I walked down the hallway, I literally looked around and asked what I was looking for. God said, "They are all gone—your assignment is over." It was time to move. I had finally learned my lessons and accomplished what God sent me there to do. Funny how we try to figure out what God is doing. When you do, it's time to start packing. It's about to be promotion time!

Literally, within weeks of hearing God's message, I was leaving to start a new job, my next assignment. Yes, it was a natural promotion too. This time I thought I was ready. No need to see that movie twice to understand the meaning. I knew I was being sent to fulfill a purpose, and I thought I was ready for battle this time. Conduit going to make something move… Another time, folks. However, just as I was leaving and excited about the new opportunity, I was reminded of something Joyce Meyer said at the time—"new levels, new devils." Let's just say I could have received four new degrees in the time it took me to complete my next assignments and learn my lessons. Some lessons are harder to learn than others, just like regular school. What can I say? Victory, the feeling of accomplishment, is so short-lived! Am I in school again? What grade is this?

Of course, it's not always easy to take the high road all the time when we face adversity. Remember, First Lady Michelle Obama said, "When they go low, we go high." It sounds simple, but trust me, it is not! As an adult, I decided long ago that I would use my mom's strategy and I would honor God by taking His high road. That meant I had to work hard to treat people the way I wanted to be treated, regardless of how they treated me. Also, my godmother in heaven showed me a long time ago that forgiveness made your heart feel ten times better than hatred and bitterness. I knew that was God's way, and I thought that was admirable enough. However, God challenged my standard by telling me that I needed to treat people the way He would treat them. Of course, He told me this while I was in the middle of battle. How do you treat people like God would, when they are treating you like the enemy would treat you? Just then the requirement was elevated times ten. It also meant that the treatment of people now had to be wrapped in loads and loads of kindness and forgiveness. Sheesh! What I also learned is that forgiveness is really for the forgiver. Trust me, you do feel better. You are also able to move on more freely, because you're not carrying someone else's baggage. That takes practice, I know.

God's change agents are often considered peculiar people, because working for God requires a response to difficulty in a manner that most people don't or won't always understand. The response God requires puzzles me sometimes too. When your conversation and actions have God as the central focus, people respond in interesting ways. However, these individuals also look specifically to see how adversity is going to be handled when they hear us say God is always the answer. When responding to adversity in an unfamiliar way, people tend to pay attention, even if it's only to say, "That's different," or "They are better than me." Hopefully, people eventually see that there is something special about the conduit and the God they serve that can't quite be explained.

My current closed-door situation was very similar with one exception: I had never been asked to make such a significant sacrifice by joining a losing team. This assignment was short-lived, and now my livelihood is in jeopardy. However, while this natural assignment has ended, I was the seed sower and protector, and a harvest was coming. Well, that's one of the reasons I find myself in this predicament. (***"A Member of the Losing Team"***—is that another book? That's 4, right?).

The Team

The leadership of a losing team of an organization is affected. Like sports, the players within an organization on a losing team are impacted too. When new leadership emerges, some players get to stay with the team; some players get traded to other teams (organizations); and the rest of the team is let go to figure it out or to make their own magic happen. The latter is the situation I found myself in—figuring it out, me and God. I know I am digressing; however, if I was so great where I was previously (you remember—great job, winning team) then why was I sent here, and why was I now facing unemployment?

As I reflect upon my **time** here, I believe many lives have been affected, and I know lots of seeds have been sown. I am a better person too. One day I am confident that there will be a great harvest. However, God does not always allow us to stick around to see the harvest, and I guess today that means me. I also met some amazing people; many of whom I am supposed to stay in contact. So I know that me coming here was initially about others, about change, and about the sown seeds. Regardless, apparently this season was concluding, and now this **time** was about me and God's purpose for my life, and that's where I needed to focus (***"Pursuit of Purpose"***—book 5?)

One of my favorite pastors would often begin her statement of fact by saying, "**One** thing was for **sure** and **two** things were for **certain**." In this instance, what I was factually **sure** of and what was definitely **certain** was that I was staring at the next chapter of my life, and right then the pages looked fuzzy and I had a lot to figure out. No matter what I could or could not see, I had faith that God had a plan. Martin Luther King Jr. said, "Faith is taking the first step even when you don't see the whole staircase."

Clearly, this season had ended. Time for me to pray, to trust God, and to **wait** for Him to reveal the signs of the beginning pages of the next chapter of the plan. I was getting excited! "But they that wait upon the Lord shall renew their strength; they shall mount up with wings as eagles; they shall run, and not be weary; and they shall walk, and not faint" (Isaiah 40:31, KJV).

The Plan

Remember, I told you that being let go was approved by God. Nothing just happens to believers. Obviously, He must have a plan. So no need to make it about anything or anyone else. Even though I really wanted to make it about a few people, today was about me and God's plan for my life because He said, "For I know the plans I have for you," declares the LORD, "plans to prosper you and not to harm you, plans to give you hope and a future" (Jeremiah 29:11 NIV).

Now, this scenario leads to several more questions for us to ponder: Was the layoff part of God's plan to point me in the direction of the next phase of my journey? Do we ever feel like you have completed an assignment or fulfilled a purpose? Does purpose in our lives ever change? Do you think the end to the season may also be the conclusion of that specific purpose? Was this a new plan, or was it the next phase of God's plan to continue the process of perfect alignment. You know when God's purpose for our lives and His plan come together. Although the coming together doesn't always feel like an amicable marriage, it sometimes feels like a collision. (An arranged marriage with someone that you don't even know.) Questions? Questions? Questions?

That's how I felt that cold December day. It was like I had just been in an accident and I was sitting in the middle of a crash. While I wasn't badly hurt, I felt momentarily dazed and confused. My purpose and my next assignment were about to collide, and it was feeling understandably uncomfortable to say the least. However, even though I was experiencing human emotion, I was not in a fretful state. Actually, I was feeling peaceful. I can't explain it. I felt like yes, I've been in an accident, but I'm only slightly injured. Maybe I've earned a little rest while I wait for answers.

To us, waiting is wasting; to GOD, waiting is working

Chapter Three

Waiting on God!

The Dash

Waiting on an answer from God is not always as easy as it sounds. Waiting for direction is even harder. Actually, I believe the waiting (the gap between the beginning and the end of **time**) is where the real lessons occur. We learn so much about God and ourselves. **Time**—"the system of those sequential relations that any event has to any other, as past, present, or future; indefinite and continuous duration regarded as that in which events succeed one another" (Dictionary.com). Our dash is the space between the day we are born and the day we die. The dash is the **time** God gives us as a gift each day. When we don't use our **time**, we lose our **time.** Think about that for a moment. Once **time** is gone, it doesn't come back. **Time** must be really special. What a rare commodity. **Time** happens so effortlessly. We expect **time** to just be, without thought. We have come so accustomed to **time** always being there. Sometimes we take it for granted.

Of course, I have questions—you're catching on. Here are my questions for you: How do you spend your gift of **time**? What does your dash look like? When you leave this earth, what will your loved ones say about your dash? How much of your **time** do you use? How much **time** do you abuse? How much of your **time** do you value? Do you treat **time** as if it's a gift from God? Just how much is your **time** worth? **("The Value of Time"—book 6?)** Questions! Questions! Questions! You know what else, a whole lot of purging, breaking, crying, learning, and growing occurs in **time**. Your dash—that space between the beginning and the end—your **time.** You're reading this book, so you still have **time. Time** for change? I used my closed-door **time** to write. If you happen to be having a closed-door experience, what are you doing right now? Get off the sidelines, and DO something for you. You have been gifted with **time**—you might as well. Life is short, so make the most of your **time**. I've bolded **time** to get on your nerves and to make a point.

The Beginning Times

We've talked about what time is and its' value. Now, let's talk about an instance when time begins, its importance, and what miracles occur in the space of time. Let me ask you to briefly think about how a baby's **time** begins in the life cycle before delivery. You have to include the woman and her body when we think about baby development too. During the process from conception to birth, the woman's body immediately starts to change from day one. While she experiences all sorts of physical changes, her emotions feel like they have been hijacked. These are the joys of pregnancy and the highs and the lows that accompany that **time** during the creation of life. Baby development happens quickly over nine months. Think about it, the life cycle in the womb is a miracle. Forty weeks later, and a baby is born from tiny cells. Now what about the wonderful labor process women get to experience, before birth. Now, admit it, during labor and delivery, you get to see some amazing events. The cycle of life—the beginning! Conception—time—delivery. That's like seed—time—harvest, right? What a **time!**

The Complicated Times

We are still talking about **time**. Don't lose sight of that fact. The closer Mom gets to delivering the baby, the more intense the pain becomes. Sounds like weathering a storm before receiving a blessing—right? As you reflect on that pain to pleasure birthing experience, I want you to also think about the complications that can accompany pregnancy. The list of complications associated with pregnancy can be soup to nuts. They can be self-imposed, treatable, and sometimes a mystery. I also want you to consider those babies born too soon and then don't survive? Born to soon…assignment aborted…hmmm.

Pay attention! What about the resistant babies? They are the overdue babies who require help to come into the world. They like their environment so much they get comfortable without knowing the wonders that lie ahead. Running out of **time**. They would rather stay, instead of being bold enough to see what's next. Stayed too long…dying on the vine. Sound familiar?

Wait, I just heard you ask, "Why are we talking about babies, creation, abortion, premature, and overdue births?" You ask a lot of questions. Okay, reflect on the cycle of life and everything connected to the process that God uses to recreate life. Now, think about God's purpose for our lives. Of course, I have several questions for you to ponder: Has a door closed in your life? Are you waiting on God to deliver you from a situation? Do you feel like you are facing uncertainty and negativity at every turn? Are you at your wits' end and experiencing such pain that you feel like you need relief like an epidural? Has it been so long that you are tired and cranky because the load is heavy? Sounds like it is almost time to **push** through! Someone is experiencing a painful **time** right now. It has been so difficult that the experience for you feels like labor pains? Push through! Do you feel like the discomfort of your current situation is similar to pregnancy symptoms—swollen feet, the back pain, and the endless trips to the bathroom that women experience during pregnancy? As the journey nears completion, those symptoms let you know the **time** is about to change and your seasons are ending and beginning. Now it's **time** to push through! Birth your vision! So "let us not become weary in doing good, for at the proper time we will reap a harvest if we do not give up" (Galatians 6:9, NIV). Don't stop now; it's about to get good. And besides, you can't quit in the middle of the race—remember.

The Seed Time

Our seeds, seasons and successes, you know seed—**time**—harvest follow the same path as that cycle of life. We plant our seeds, and in **time** the seeds are nurtured and protected from harm. In **time,** some of us may even get the honor of protecting someone else's seeds. Until this moment, I did not count it all joy to have to cultivate someone else's seed. Ever been a surrogate? It's the **time** we need to talk about while we are ***carrying our next purpose.*** WOW! That even blew me away as I wrote that. Say it...another book (*"**Carrying Purpose**"* number 8). However, "The harvest is plentiful, but the workers are few" (Matthew 9:37 NIV). That plentiful harvest must be delivered, or it dies. Someone has to carry the seeds through to harvest. If the workers are limited, then that means someone has to pick up the slack. Are you wondering why you feel so full all the time? You better plant more seeds and then develop more workers to lighten your load. What is that? I think it's called witnessing—ha ha!

The Vision

What happens to God's vision if we try to get rid of the load and give up? That's like being seven months pregnant and deciding to quit. Think about the job you left because of difficult people? Did you abort the mission? Did you cause your own door to close? You quit, just before giving birth to your dream or vision right in the midst of hard labor. I know the final stages of labor were difficult. That's also an indicator that you are almost at the end. In times like these, we need the Savior. Hold on, the ride is about to get bumpy. Trust God!

Did you give up too soon because it was painful and uncomfortable for you? So what happened to those visions that died in the womb? The prematurely closed door. Prayerfully we get another chance. What about those births that never get delivered simply because God's vision was too big to comprehend? (***"Afraid to Move"*** **book 7?)** Their environment will eventually dry up and become devoid of resources needed to survive. The vision ceases to grow and cannot produce. Do you feel like you are currently having a desert experience? Maybe you've been there too long. Do you think maybe it is time to move? Trust God! "Ask, and it will be given you; seek and ye will find; knock, and the door will be opened for you" (Matthew 7:7, NIV). You must allow yourself to dream big!

Are you waiting on God? Perhaps God is waiting on you. Now maybe it's **time** for you to get ready to birth a new vision? Labor pains—it's **time** to prepare for delivery! Wait now, can't push too soon. No premature deliveries here! **Time** to PUSH? (**P**ray **U**ntil **S**omething **H**appens!) Someone needs to get ready to PUSH right now! If it's you, bear down now and PUSH. Push through the labor, and deliver that purpose! The greater your challenge, the bigger your blessing! Your breakthrough is here—it's **time** to harvest your crop! Push! Push! Push! Congratulations, you just birthed your next purpose! It might feel just like delivering a ten-pound baby. While you may be tired and a little tattered, that has to feel pretty amazing! Get some rest; you've earned it. My apologies if that was not for you. It was for someone, and they really needed a release. Let's celebrate with them! That was exhausting. I'm excited for you, but I'm tired too! Okay, let's get back. Where were we?

Wasted Time

Back to time. Reflect on the endless amounts of **time** that you have wasted over your life thus far. What dreams and visions have not come to fruition because you have been stuck? Yes, I've wasted a lot of my **time** too. I also feel like I have had more than my fair share of stress built into my **time.** Of course, we all feel like that, I'm sure. However, what **time** has taught me is that the more I trust God, the less I experience prolonged periods of stress. Trust me—life is so much sweeter with God. When there is less stress, there is less chaos and a lot less uncertainty. I can find peace trusting God even though currently, I was facing the unknown. I didn't say no stress and chaos; I said a lot less. Don't miss that! Since our lives revolve around **time,** we must learn how to embrace the **time** that God gives us and wait! What **time** is it for you? Was it **time** for me to give birth to new purpose? What **time** is it? "There is a time for everything, and a season for every activity under the heavens" (Ecclesiastes 3:1, NIV). No rest for the weary!

The Harvested Time

What about me? Am I about to give birth to a dream or a new vision? I feel like I am empty and full at the same **time**. Does that make sense? I feel empty because a door has closed. I also have a feeling of expectation because a door has closed, as I have no idea what tomorrow holds. I am really excited about tomorrow though. I am looking forward to experiencing the next phase of God's plan for me.

I think about the seeds God has allowed me to sow. What does the harvest look like from those seeds? I also think about the seeds I was charged to protect. Have your harvests been plentiful? As I reflect, I always seem to enjoy harvest after difficulty—you know, like sunshine after the rain. The labor is excruciating, and then the blessing of a new baby. Pain before pleasure—wasn't that a song? However, I will "trust in the LORD with all [my] heart **and do not lean** on [my] own understanding. In all [my] ways acknowledge Him, And He will make [my] paths straight" (Proverbs 3:5–6 ESV). God's Word is truth, and it is surely liberating. Today I needed to stand on that truth. While this road ahead was momentarily dark, I knew it was only temporary. Of course, lies of failure were being presented to me. However, I was comforted and excited by the fact that in Deuteronomy 31:16 NIV, God said for me *not to be* two things: "Do not be ***afraid*** *or* ***terrified*** because of them, for the LORD your God goes with you; he will never leave you nor forsake you." However, He did say for me *to be* two things, and that is to "be strong and courageous" (Deuteronomy 31:16, NIV). **Time** is filled with swift transition, which is why we must always be ready; that includes being ready to swing at the curve-balls too.

The Transition Time

Do you know that life's disappointments can become God's appointments if you trust Him? You know, when He turns obstacles into opportunities, pain into possibilities, turmoil into triumph. Okay, okay, you get it—right? And besides, if life was wonderful all the **time**, would we need to trust God so much? While this **time** was foreign to me and uncomfortable, I was trusting God! I wasn't about to move too quickly though. I was waiting on God's direction.

Experience has taught me to wait on God. How many times have we heard, been told again, repeated it ourselves, and sung a few songs that have even been written about it—experience? It's the best teacher. Remember, you must know God for yourself. I need to do something though. Even though time is filled with swift transition and much uncertainty, we must remember to trust God always. No sudden moves though; remember, I'm carrying purpose, and I feel like I'm getting ready to PUSH! Does anybody have any pain reliever?

Waiting on God!
Not easy but worth it!!

"TRUST IN THE LORD WITH ALL YOUR HEART,
AND LEAN NOT ON YOUR OWN UNDERSTANDING;
IN ALL YOUR WAYS ACKNOWLEDGE HIM,
AND HE SHALL DIRECT YOUR PATHS."
PROVERBS 3:5–6

Chapter Four

Trusting God

The Waiting

Waiting on God during this **time** does not mean we sit and do nothing. That's like needing a job and sitting home waiting for the job to knock on the door just because you have faith in God. If you don't get out and complete applications, network, and attend job fairs, etc., the chances are slim that a job is going to knock on your front door. I'm not saying that doesn't happen. Many people have received job offers when they weren't looking for a job at the **time**. Clearly, I did not apply, nor was I looking for this temporary job! Somehow it found me anyway. So we improve our chances for success when we work at it, and God will reward our diligence and our faith. Stop wasting your **time.** There's that word again. It's just like the news van! Many of us have had love ones who have gone on to glory. Most of us wish we had more **time** with them. I know I do. **Time** is rare and precious. It's more valuable than we realize—don't forget to treat time like a gift!

For us to mature and grow spiritually, we must really learn to rely on and trust God more. Are you willing to follow God, embrace the journey and enjoy the ride? We can admit our flaws and apologize when we're wrong. We realize that while we strive for excellence, life happens. We must not only be able to adapt, we must be willing to adjust and know that we are not perfect. Our experiences (good and bad) encourage us to trust God more. Someone said mistakes are the best lessons, while experience is the best teacher. Do you agree? We also begin to understand that these experiences are what shape our testimonies. This is how we become God's example. It's like advertisement. We help others when we are transparent and open about our faith in God. Our testimonies are one of His marketing tools. For those of us who have a need to always be in control, this will be a difficult task at first. However, once we relinquish control, God can move and that becomes our testimony. It's also how our faith is built. Remember the song lyrics by Edward Mote: "My hope is built on nothing less than Jesus Christ, my righteousness; on Christ the solid rock I stand; all other ground is sinking sand."

Our Faith

We must seek God so we can actually experience His fullness in all His awesome splendor. If you really want to experience the power of God, then it's **time** to go deeper. His desire is to see us work at our faith. He wants us to show Him with confidence that we not only have faith and trust in Him when our needs are met, and life is great. God really wants to know that we also trust Him in our **time** of need and/or trouble. He wants us to acknowledge our dependence upon Him. When the **time** appears to be darkest, do you try God first? I know it's easy to trust God when we feel safe and our bills are paid. We say we trust God when we have food to eat and a warm place to sleep. What happens when any one of those things are threatened? What happens to our faith? Don't you know that when we are at a **time** when we need him most, that's when God shows out! God wants us to not just say that we trust him. He wants to know that we believe like we know our name and that God has our back. Now that's faith! "For as the body without the spirit is dead, so faith without works is dead also" (James 2:26 KJV). Get your grind on!

You must plan your work; and work your plan people. Make the most of your **time**. Treat it like gold! Take advantage of the **time** God has given. Great preparation while you wait within your **time**.

The door has closed anyway. What are you doing right now with your **time**? I encourage you to seek God who knows your deeds. Put your faith in he who has placed before you an open door that no one can shut; (Revelations 3:8, NIV). I am standing on the promises of God! On Christ the solid rock I stand; all other ground is sinking sand. What are you standing on? No matter how big the problem may be, God is bigger. "Now to him who is able to do immeasurably more than all we ask or imagine, according to his power that is at work within us" (Ephesians 3:20, NIV). This journey is all about faith!

The Experience

I have the faith that I do because of my **time** with God. Remember, we said experience is the best teacher. My score is like 10,000 to 0, probably more—where God has never let me down. Now, I won't say that every answered prayer was to my liking; but just like us as natural parents, our children aren't always pleased with us or our decisions all the **time** either—but they do trust us because we consistently demonstrate over **time** our genuine love and concern for them. When God has consistently been faithful over **time,** why would we doubt Him when we have a problem or concern regardless of the magnitude? "And if God cares so wonderfully for wildflowers that are here today and thrown into the fire tomorrow, he will certainly care for you. Why do you have so little faith?" (Matthew 6:30, NLT).

During times of trouble (the closed door) we need to be able to hear from God and be able to receive his guidance and direction from the Word. During your **time**, everyone from everywhere will be offering advice. Sometimes that's just designed to continue the distraction. If you don't know who the author of confusion and chaos is, you better learn quickly because your life could depend on it. So, "be still, and know that I am God!" (Psalms 46:10 NIV). This feels like an appropriate time for me to **refresh, fast and pray.** Even though I know all this, I still have a lot to figure out. I'm peeking through the window curtains looking to see if I can find out what God is doing.

Remember, one thing is for **sure** and two things are for **certain,** we may be caught off guard, but God never is. It's all about His plan, His time, and our actions while we wait and carry out the purpose. Sometimes there is a significant difference between our plans and God's purpose. "Many are the plans in a person's heart, but it is the LORD's purpose that prevails" (Proverbs 19:21, NIV).

I believe our plans are our dreams, our visions, and our ideas that originate from within. They are shaped by the people and circumstances we encounter. However, I also believe God's plan is what He intends to happen in our lives. God's plan is always perfect, and of course, it always prevails, even when it doesn't always seem to make sense. No, His plan does not always fit so nicely within our plan. This closed-door situation I currently find myself in was no exception. I thought the plan was for me to remain where I was and to continue to impact and influence. While the latter might be true, it was painfully obvious that my plans were definitely contrary to God's plan. Today's events appear to be designed to enable God's purpose to prevail. "And we know that all things work together for good to those who love God, to those who are called according to His purpose" (Romans 8:28 NIV). So, God is still in control, and I am trusting Him! However, if you don't know Him, it will be impossible for you to trust him. He has a plan, I'm sure of it. No coincidences here, I know God.

"For I know the plans I have for you, declares the Lord, plans to prosper you and not to harm you, plans to give you hope and a future" (Jeremiah 29:11, NIV).

I have a plan.
Do you trust me?
—God

Faith is not believing that God can,

It's knowing that God will.

Chapter Five

Knowing God

Heaven Is Never in Chaos!

Know God—no chaos; no God—know chaos! Would you say the opposite of chaos is control? Do you believe that God is always in control? Can you imagine heaven being in a catastrophic state littered with unforeseen events? Last question—Do you believe God uses the most difficult circumstances for our good and His glory? I believe what starts out as chaos soon transitions into control, and if we calm our emotions long enough to hear from God. "And we know [with confidence] that in all things God works for the good of those who love Him, who have been called according to His purpose" *(Romans 8:28, NIV).*

You must recognize the chaos and make a conscious decision not to allow it to consume you. Our faith in God helps with this process. I've discovered that every situation that causes pain, also comes with purpose. Would you choose to intentionally cause your child harm? Of course not! However, you would allow your child to make his/her own mistakes—right? How else do they learn? If you look closely enough at chaos, you will see that the chaos is wrapped in God's love just like a present. The stress comes when we miss the gift because it isn't packaged the way we want it wrapped.

What do I mean by that? Suppose you are looking for a mate. You meet someone wonderful, but according to you, they are not handsome enough or smart enough. Turns out that was the perfect mate for you, but you couldn't see the gift inside because you were too busy looking at the package and not the gift. Now who is this for today?

I believe if we paid closer attention, we would stress so much less. We also wouldn't be so easily knocked off our center. I think some challenges are designed to make us stronger, or at a minimum to help us to see the strength we possess on the inside. How do we really know how strong we are or what we are capable of, if we are not tested every now and then? It's like taking a class; how do we demonstrate mastery of course content? We take a test.

I believe God's test are more about Him showing us our strength in addition to allowing us to see what we have learned. Often, we don't know how strong we are until we need strength. Sometimes we surprise ourselves. Ever said, "I didn't know my own strength"?

No Surprises Here!

We have always heard that God never makes a mistake and His plan is deliberate. Do you believe that? I do, I believe that everything with God is purposeful and part of a plan. He is never surprised by anything or anyone in the life of His child. After all, if God is omniscient, then He is all-knowing. It's hard to be surprised when you know everything—right? I believe when we experience a painful situation, we focus on the symptoms of pain, and often we ignore why we are in pain. We let the condition go untreated as we focus on the symptoms. God might be trying to get our attention. Through fasting, praying, and studying God's Word, we can go to Him, get help, self-reflect, and recover. Just like physical pain, if we allow the condition to go untreated, it gets worse and becomes more painful. If you are currently experiencing a closed-door situation, let me ask you this: Have you gone to where you know peace and comfort lies—at the throne of grace where God resides? Have you been obedient in the things God has asked of you?

Again, ask for God's help, self-reflect, and fix the problem. You may have to allow Him to work it out, and that is not always an easy, quick fix. However, if we remember the situation is either sent our way directly by God or with His permission, I believe we will look to God sooner for help. I also believe we won't stress so easily. This means we can focus sooner and ask for the help we need. Ultimately, our charge is to figure out how to be content in the space that we are in because it's all part of God's plan. "I am not saying this because I am in need, for I have learned to be content whatever the circumstances. I know what it is to have plenty. I have learned the secret of being content in any and every situation; whether well fed or hungry, whether living in plenty or in want. I can do all things through him who gives me strength" (Philippians 4:11–13 NIV). We have to depend on God when we can't depend on ourselves. God is our partner in this journey called life! Do you trust Him?

A Good Hand!

Regardless of the closed-door situation I find myself in today, I am content. I know with confidence that God has a plan and is working it out. I know He only wants what's best for me. Even though I am slightly caught off guard, I must remember that God is never surprised. And yes, I trust Him.

Sometimes you have to look at situations and how we respond to them, like a good game of spades. In the card game, no matter how much complaining we do about the cards we receive, they don't change, and we don't get new cards until the next hand. Spades is about the cards you're dealt, but it is also a game of strategy. When we get lousy cards, we are required to play the hand and rely on our partner to pick up the slack. Now, I'm sure you caught that. For us as believers, we have the best spade partner ever. He knows the game and is the best strategist. With odds like that, we simply can't and won't lose! We will lose a hand or two—that's just the law of probability. So again, we must learn to be content, even during the wilderness experience. We must also be okay with the help God provides. I was trying to move on, but we need to stay here a bit longer because obviously there is more to say.

I think I need to say that again. Think about how much we pout, hold our breath, be in denial, or act like Alise on the *Diary of a Mad Black Woman* movie. You remember the scene: her fingernails were being peeled from the door as she was being put out and forced to leave. Whatever cards have been dealt to you this round—trust your partner! Anyway, acting out never changes the cards, and we are not trusting God if we are acting like a fool! Excuse me if this is not for you. Trust me, it's for somebody! The next question is, How do you be content with the cards? Remember, they are temporary. Yes, you might lose a round or two and get set even (still talking spades). What I do know is that you will get new cards; I promise. Trust your partner and say yes to His process. Alise was blessed in the end, right! She had to go through it to get to it!!! Even the rain cloud has to eventually move. So you might as well dance in the rain! Be content…

Contentment

Okay, let's talk about contentment. Can you say JOB? Not job like work, silly—Job in the Bible who teaches us about suffering, the tactics of the enemy, and then faith and trust in God. At least that's what I learned thirty years ago when God kept sending me back to read Job when I was dealing with an extremely difficult situation. We must pay attention, stay prayerful, and embrace the difficulties of life because we really don't always know what God is planning. "Do not be anxious about anything, but in every situation, by prayer and petition, with thanksgiving, present your requests to God." (Philippians 4:6, NIV). Remember I told you that I have learned to be content in whatever state I am in. When we know God, we have confidence that while we don't know what God must do to answer our prayers (especially the specific ones), we know that we will get an answer. Waiting on God is the hard part. Remember, to us, waiting is wasting **time**. To God, waiting is working in **time**.

Thirty years later, now God takes me to the book of Daniel to provide encouragement during the difficult days. Yes, if God can preserve the three Hebrew boys from harm in the fiery furnace, surely He will protect me and you. Talk about a seemingly closed-door experience. Refresh yourself and reread the book of Daniel. Remember, not only were Daniel's friends spared death in the fiery furnace, the captors were burned by their excessive heat meant to destroy their prisoners. Look at God: the prisoners survived, and the captors perished. The famous Bible story of Daniel and the lion's den is more than a simple account of God's deliverance. It also shows that no one or nothing is a match for the true God. You know we say it, but do we believe it—"what the enemy means as a setback, God will use that same scenario as a setup for a blessing"? Daniel and the three Hebrew boys are great examples of orchestrated setbacks transformed into setups for blessings. Be content in the space that we're in. No matter what kind of closed-door situation we find ourselves in, God is always there with us and for us. So, pray and be specific. He's right there, and He is listening. However, remember special prayers take longer to answer.

Special Orders

How often do your prayers come with specific requests? The special prayers. Ever wonder why some prayers get answered sooner than others? I still ask, Why does God answer some prayers immediately, while other prayers take time? What about the prayers with specificity, which feel like the answers take a lifetime? I think specific prayers are like the special orders we place at our favorite restaurant. Special orders are items not immediately found on the regular menu. You know the meal we want prepared in a way that's different from what's advertised on the menu. I am famous for changing items, adding ingredients and spices so I get the perfect meal for me that day. What happens when we place those special orders? We must wait a little longer! And you know what, we wait with great expectation of receiving our special order. We are also oblivious to the preparation between our request/petition being placed, and us receiving the order/blessing. What we know is, it is coming! Do you know God well enough to believe in faith that He is coming to see about you too?

One Sunday, an elder preached about prayer and protection. During his message, he referred to a scene from the movie *Conan the Destroyer*. Conan was hanging from a rope with one hand, and he was holding his sword with his other hand destroying his enemies. Using this illustration, the elder said, sometimes God's battles on our behalf can be just that intense. We are usually unaware of it all, and it happens while we are waiting on God. Do you trust him? Will you wait with confidence? Sometimes, for God to answer prayers He has to make moves like chess. More specific prayers require more deliberate moves. I recently witnessed a prayer request being answered three years later. God had to be both strategic and deliberate in His plan. The answer was ultimately perfect; however, His strategy included countless moves for His plan to work out perfectly. Specific prayers require patience. "Wait for the LORD; be strong, and let your heart take courage; wait for the LORD! (Psalm 27:14, ESV)

God's Plan

Now stop and think of the number of times God has delayed or denied a prayer request or just completely derailed our perfect plan. Did it feel like a closed door? Of course, it's always something we really wanted. Later we realize that the denial or delay was simply God's protection from what was coming that we knew nothing about. That was a closed door! Learning to trust God is a process. Remember, though, He is the dependable parent. As parents, sometimes we have to say no to our children.

We all have one of these stories. "I was stuck in traffic and just missed that car accident." That company went bankrupt, I'm so glad I didn't get that job." "We lost the bid on the house we thought we wanted, until we looked further and found the house that stole our hearts." Trust Him sooner without thinking, like breathing. Besides, worry does not influence outcome. Worry a little, or worry a lot, we get the same outcome. My other favorite pastor would say, "If you're praying, why are you worrying? And if you are worrying, why are you praying? Hmmm. Save yourself stress and strife by trusting God sooner than later. We spend too much time trying to make a beautiful picture out of broken or damaged pieces in our lives that no longer fit. "Cast your cares on the Lord and he will sustain you; he will never let the righteous be shaken" (Psalm 55:22 NIV). Belonging to God also means God shares our burdens. We may not get an immediate response. Sometimes, things get worse before they get better—trust is still required. God always takes care of us. Timing might be the issue; however, we should find comfort knowing that God is with us even in our suffering and He always has the final word.

The Shattered Pieces

Only God can take the shattered pieces of our lives and put them back together and make something beautiful, even better, out of each damaged piece. The key is to surrender the broken pieces to God sooner than later. What amazes me is what He can do with brokenness, in some instances that were intentionally discarded by others. Who went through the worst divorce, only now to be happily married again? Sometimes the door has to close. This is exactly why we have to trust God. What about the pieces like self-doubt, low self-esteem, disappointment, and discouragement.? Do yourself a favor and give those broken pieces to God right now and wait and see what He does with them. You're not doing anything with them anyway.

Now, I want you to think back for a moment when you experienced pain or difficulty, or you simply felt broken. Prayerfully, that experience is easier to look back on now because, you gave it to God and He took care of the situation in His own way and in His time. I'm sure some of you are reflecting on real pain. The kind of pain where you absolutely did not think you would ever recover. Now, if you really gave it to God—I know you are better. If not, then you haven't given it all to God with all your heart. Because when you really give it to God, you have to give Him the pain that you are carrying too. I know some things are easier to move from than others. I get that. My prayer is that God has comforted you and given you peace in your heart to say today is better than yesterday and the day before that too. "Therefore humble yourselves under the mighty hand of God, that He may exalt you in due time, casting all your care upon Him, for He cares for you" (1 Peter 5:6–7 NKJV).

The Release

If you think about it, casting your cares means asking for help. The difficulty I have found is some people view seeking help as a sign of weakness or even an admission of failure. I know it's hard for us to ask for help because we are always accustomed to handling our own business with little or no assistance from others. We feel powerful and confident—right? Nothing is worse than having problems with no means to solve them. This scenario makes this point even more important.

Casting/giving your cares, admitting that you need help requires humility, and God also gives grace to the humble which is a bonus. That's why God commands us to humble ourselves first and then cast our cares on Him. *To cast* means "to throw." Imagine you're walking along and kids are playing with a ball that rolls your way. Most of us will pick up the ball, throw it back, and keep walking. We would not wait around to see what the kids did with the ball. We would throw the ball and keep walking. The kids weren't playing with us, and it isn't our ball—remember? It's not yours so throw it back… Did you get that? He did say cast it…Come on now, humble yourself, ask for help and then just throw it to Him—right now!

I dare you to toss your problem, your worry, or your concern to God right now and keeping walking. It's not yours to begin with anyway, remember? He told you to do it, so do it and do it now! Give all those cares back to the rightful owner because He cares for you! Release it and let it go! Place your cares in a box, put the box on a boat, and watch the boat sail into the sunset carrying your cares away.

Letting go means literally opening our hands. It also means actually opening our hearts too for God to do His best work. I imagine we all have had some sort of shock or devastation to our system where we didn't know how we would recover. Someone immediately comes to my mind as I reflect on my own journey. I won't share the particulars of their story. What I will say is, I witnessed their pain from afar. It was the kind of pain that made your own heart ache for the individual. The pain was obvious on their face and evident in their heart. I won't say this is a situation where life is better for them. I will say their life is now on a trajectory that they may not have otherwise thought about for themselves. This individual is now doing things I'm sure they never thought imaginable. Learning to trust God when the pain is unbearable is about relationship. I witnessed restoration!

Now when I see them, I see peace on their face and happiness in their heart. Their today is amazing, and it is only possible because of the incredibly painful door that closed yesterday. I know they trust God. I know this because every time I saw them during those difficult days, that's what they would tell me. I don't know if today would have been possible but for their painful yesterday. Not that they weren't making a difference before, but today they are really making a difference. They are touching so many more lives and representing God in such a major way. Watching God is hard to comprehend sometimes. God is still able, y'all believe that! "Now to Him who is able to do exceedingly abundantly above all that we ask or think, according to the power that works in us..." (Ephesians 3:20–21, NKJV).

I have such a greater appreciation for really understanding that it truly is better to love and lose love than to have never experienced love at all. My point is, I have seen, and I have had many instances where the sun could not shine if the rain (whatever it is) had not happened. Give it to God sooner because the Potter wants to put us back together again. "But now, O LORD, you are our Father; we are the clay, and you are our potter; we are all the work of your hand" (Isaiah 64:8, ESV). Remember the lyrics to "The Potter's House"... "Dreams and visions shattered, you're all broken inside. You don't have to stay in the shape that you're in; The Potter wants to put you back together again." We are right where God wants you and me to be.

During our closed-door experiences, He patiently waits for us to turn to Him and let go of **IT!** Whatever **IT** is in your life. Trust Him to give you strength for the season. What freedom we feel when we can actually trust God enough to give our painful situations to Him immediately. In our silliness, we try to help God. Ha! For us to give it to God, we first must let it go! You know, let go and let God! Remember, no one loves us the way God does—**unconditionally!** With faith, we would enjoy our time more if we think of God as the answer sooner to meet whatever need we have and resolve whatever issues we have today. Give God the hard stuff, all of it. The ugly stuff too. God wants us to have faith in Him, no matter what.

Our Faith

"Now faith is the substance of things hoped for, the evidence of things not seen" (Hebrews 11:1 KJV). We are all confident of our faith in God when things are going well and our needs are met—right? Do you feel equally as confident about your faith in God when you are troubled or in need of help?

Well, if we confess to know Christ and say we are a child of the King of Kings and Lord of Lords, we need to be able to demonstrate our faith by showing the true power of God during any closed-door situation. Remember, people are always watching how we handle adversity. How do you market God to others? You do know that we are the best part of God's marketing plan. Through our everyday living, we are supposed to show others what the benefits of working for the company of GOD look like. Not just on Sunday… So are you bearing good fruit for inspection? God said, "I am the vine; you are the branches. If you remain in me and I in you, you will bear much fruit; apart from me you can do nothing" (John 15:5, NIV).

If God is the vine and we are the branches, then think about our children. We are their vine, and they are our branches. Our kids are dependent on us just as we are dependent on God. We are responsible for developing their brains. They depend on their vines for nourishment, guidance, direction, and pruning so they can grow. Are you taking care of your vines in order to produce strong branches so they can produce good fruit? Do you provide good soil to grow good fruit? Poor vines produce branches that produce poor fruit. That's why we have to take care of ourselves so that we may produce great fruit. This extends beyond our natural children too.

Our vines carry the required good nutrients that are passed along to allow us to grow good branches in order to produce good fruit. Sucker shoots are the mechanisms vines use to carry their nutrients. If your sucker shoots are clogged with sludge like an artery for the heart, the chances of you producing good fruit are slim. Are you bearing good fruit, or are you clogged with stinking thinking and mess, preventing you from bearing great fruit? The fruit inspector is watching. Take a break; that was a lot to process. **Time to reflect...**

Whether you realize it or not,
People are watching you. Even in
Small places, make sure you're
Representing God in a Great way!!!

Chapter Six

Representing God

The Clogged Sucker Shoots

Let's talk about tree anatomy for a moment. Naturally, fruit gets its nutrients through the vines that are connected to the tree. What's inside the vine is passed onto the branches. If the branch is unable to receive the nutrients from the vine, we get bad fruit. Bad tree branches will either bear rotten fruit or no fruit at all. It's about the sucker shoots. A vine left to itself, produces what are called "sucker shoots." Suckers are vigorous, vertical growth coming from the roots or lower main stem of a plant. Suckers are usually considered undesirable—you want the plant, but you don't want its sucker because they sap the plant's energy (https://thespruce.com/ways-to-control-plant suckers-3269528). As they grow larger, they begin to do exactly what their name suggests: they suck away the life-giving sap on its way from the vine to the branch. Before long, the branch becomes malnourished and eventually dies, all because the sucker shoot would consume what was originally intended for the branch. Sucker shoots will never bear fruit. They will grow leaves abundantly, but they will never produce fruit. From the distance, they look like they belong. Remind you of anybody? They will only greatly reduce the quantity and quality of fruit the true branches can bear. "Either make the tree good and its fruit good; or make the tree bad and its fruit bad; for the tree is known by its fruit" (Matthew 12:33, ESV). What is the key to bearing great fruit as a Believer? Naturally, fruit comes from a healthy plant production. In God's Word, fruit is often referred to as a person's outward actions that occurs because of the condition of his/her heart. Jesus was very clear in communicating what we must do to bear good fruit. He said apart from Him we can do nothing. We get our strength from God. So, our connectivity is crucial to our existence. The tree branch gets its strength, nourishment, protection and energy from the vine. We too must be feeding our spirit with God's Word and consistent prayer. God knows what He has given to each of us. He also has expectations of what we do with what is given. He replied, "Well done, good and faithful servant! You have been faithful with a few things; I will put you in charge of many things." (Matthew 25:21 NIV).

Pruning (literally meaning "to cleanse") also removes the dirt, cobwebs, dried leaves, and fungus that has collected in order to make way for new fruit. Just like regular trees, we need spiritual pruning too. Jesus reminds us of this when He says, "I am the true vine, and my Father is the vinedresser. Every branch in Me that does not bear fruit He takes away; and every branch that bears fruit He prunes, that it might bear more fruit" (John 15:1–2, NKJV). You can look at a hundred vines and you will never see one branch pruning another branch! It seems to me that the job of pruning, shaping, and otherwise trimming those vines must be the job of someone besides the branches themselves. According to starkbros.com fruit trees left unpruned may struggle to grow. Trees that are unpruned actually take longer to bear fruit. A tree needs pruning to help it survive planting. Pruning is the key to getting a new fruit tree off to a great start (www.starkbros.com/growing-guide/article/successful-tree-pruning). It is clear that the responsibility for pruning is left to God. What exactly is this fruit that God is expecting from us?

Are you feeling weak and drained? Perhaps you're growing weary. If there is nothing physically wrong that may be causing these feelings, then maybe it's **time** to ask God to show you the sucker shoots that are clogged and zapping the abundant life and strength from you that He intended you to have! Allow Him to prune you!

This may mean getting rid of some old habits. As good as we may think we are, thoughts, attitudes, or behaviors need to die so that we may live. Through the power of God, even more fruit will be produced in our lives—just like the trees. This is not usually a pleasant process. As people, we tend to cling to our human condition and understanding, and the things we deem to be important in this life (careers, social standing, financial security, 'church' status, etc.). If we are not willing to suffer the loss of "all these things," it's a pretty good indicator we are not depending on the true vine as our life source. The article "*Why Does Food Rot?*" tells us that when fruit is harvested, it is detached from its life source. In other words, once the fruit is picked, it begins to die immediately. I'm thankful that our spiritual fruit is not like natural fruit.

The things we are in need of start and end with us staying connected to the true vine, Christ Jesus. You have to really experience God in order to then be able to produce great fruit. Just as fruit is unique to its tree, our fruit is unique to us. "You did not choose me, but I chose you and appointed you so that you might go and bear fruit—fruit that will last—and so that whatever you ask in my name the Father will give you (John 15:16, NIV). Similar to the vine being the nutrient source for fruit, the heart begins and ends as the life source for our human bodies. Our lives begin and end with a heartbeat. With each heartbeat, the heart circulates blood throughout the body. Unlike God, there is nothing we can do. The heart is our life source from the beginning, and we are not able to do much without our heart. When something changes with our heart rhythm, we notice immediately because we know our heart. If we want to live a long life, being heart-healthy is important. When we take care of our heart, our heart takes care of us. Likewise, God, too, is like our heart. We can do nothing without Him, and with Him all things are possible. We have to spend time with God, getting to know Him. We should want to become familiar with the sound of His voice, abiding in His presence, all day every day. Reading the Word often allows us to steadily draw from His unfailing wisdom, and the Bible is our life's road map. Every answer we need is contained in the Word. That's why it's my favorite book. I especially enjoy the revelations we receive when we are willing to take a deeper dive into the Word. The Apostle Paul shares with us the fruit that the vinedresser expects from us, "the fruits of the Spirit" (that which the Spirit produces) "is love, joy, peace, long-suffering, gentleness, goodness, faithfulness, meekness, self-control," nine qualities gathered as one cluster, just as a grapevine produces.

The whole point to our existence as believers is to show others the way to Christ through our daily living. We shouldn't have to wear a big cross and say "Jesus" three or four times in every sentence for others to know we serve God. Representing God should be natural. "Remain in me, as I also remain in you. No branch can bear fruit by itself; it must remain in the vine. Neither can you bear fruit unless you remain in me" (John 15:4, NIV). This is our job as believers.

If you have accepted your job as a believer then you have been hired by heaven and God's benefits are out of this world! (Yup, another book—**"Earning God's Benefits"**—idk, book 8?) Our job is to show God and His love by the fruit we bear. Can you identify the tree by the fruit it bears? Or maybe the question is, Do people know us by the fruit we bear? You know an apple comes from an apple tree, right? You know oranges come from an orange tree. Does your fruit look like it comes from God's tree of life?

Look over your field for a moment to visualize what it might look like because of the many seeds sown. What does your harvest look like? Have you sown good seeds to reap a great fruit harvest? Test your fruit to ensure your sucker shoots are open and free from debris to produce good fruit before God does. Fruit is used as the metaphor to describe our own produce. Our fruit is the direct result of whatever controls our hearts. The fruit of the Spirit is where true fruitfulness begins. What happens as a result of our spiritual fruitfulness is God is glorified, we grow, and disciples are born. His desire is "For those God foreknew he also predestined to be conformed to the image of his Son, that he might be the first born among many brothers and sisters. And those he predestined, he also called; those he called, he also justified; those he justified, he also glorified." (Romans 29–30 NIV). We are expected to be as...

GOD CREATED
MAN IN HIS
OWN IMAGE

"Let us not become weary in doing good, for at the proper time we will reap a harvest if we do not give up."
—Galatians 6:9

Chapter Seven

Harvesting for God

The Test

We know testimonies come from tests. Promotions do too, but we must be ready. We know that tests can be difficult if we have not studied to prepare ourselves. Being ill-equipped (lacking knowledge or skill) for the task at hand can make for a tough time too. By reading God's Word, and learning from past experiences, we should be able to pass our tests and get promoted to the next level in Christ. I recognize some tests are harder to pass than others, just like school. A long time ago, I remember Joyce Meyer said, "New levels—new devils." I'm just saying. We don't get off that easy. "From everyone who has been given much, much will be demanded; and from the one who has been entrusted with much, much more will be asked" (Luke 12:48, NIV). Your fruit and/or your harvest is being tested. Will your fruit be able to weather the storms of life, no matter what the circumstance? It's raining somewhere. Protect your seeds, and do not let them get washed away. Are you on your post? You're being tested...

The Recycle Grade

Now, if you are wondering why you keep finding yourself in the same situation over and over, maybe you're being tested and perhaps you keep failing the test. Do you keep encountering the same closed doors? You do know, that repeating the same behavior and expecting different results is the definition of insanity—right? Are you asking why you haven't heard from God in a while regarding this recurring situation? Well, could it be because the teacher typically doesn't offer help during a test. Have you studied and/or learned from your past experiences? Can you demonstrate your knowledge and maturity regarding the topic or situation? If the answer is no, you will be receiving the regrettable "R" grade for **RECYCLE**. "R" also stands for **REPEAT!**

However, unlike life, God is always willing to offer another opportunity. Typically, you don't fail and it's over. However, you will have to repeat the sometimes-painful experience to figure out the question, so you can discover the answer, so you can get promoted. Did you get that? It's like trying to skip steps in baby labor. Unfortunately, like school, you will not be able to go to the next level until you master what God has for you to learn or eliminate in the current level. Time to stop staring at the door!

Some of y'all been sitting in the same class for ten years! Come on now! I know the feeling. Remember I told you that one of my assignments lasted sixteen years. The primary lesson was learning how to fight without my fists. Your fists can't help you when you're fighting in spiritual warfare. You know, hold my peace and let the Lord fight my battle. The door kept closing, and I kept fighting. What was that insanity definition again? Obviously, for many of those years I thought God needed my help. You hurt me, my first instinct is to hurt back. Well, it was my first instinct. Now it's all about love. I had to unlearn my way and relearn God's way. Let's say learning is a slow and sometimes-painful process. I remember that experience very vividly. When the situation got to be way too painful, I recall crying out to God for help and me telling Him that I was tired of fighting. His response to me was "about time—I've been waiting for you to get tired of fighting in your own strength." When I stopped fighting them, even though they were still fighting me, I literally witnessed a paradigm shift in the atmosphere. It was another one of my more memorable experiences with God. All that

I am sharing with you is a lifetime of testimony. Didn't we say that experience was the best teacher. Remember, I told you that I was not in a fretful state—now you know why. Score—10,000 to 0. God is always winning! Now that's some good fruit.

I believe our experiences are foundational. We are also supposed to learn and pay it forward. We must keep adding to the surface to ensure the foundation is solid. We can't build anything on a weak surface. Try to build a house on a weak, unstable foundation. Would we ever build a house on a foundation made of sand? Of course not! Remember...on Christ the solid rock we stand—all other ground is sinking sand! Fix the cracks in your foundation to avoid the dreaded recycle grade. We have work to do. Are we still talking about closed doors?

The Diet

Today do you find yourself in a recycled state—a closed door? If so, ask yourself these questions... What have I learned about myself, and what have I learned about God? What is God trying to teach me? More importantly, what is it that I need to purge from myself? I need to shed the baggage associated with the deadweight experience and be ready to soar to new heights. We can't soar like an eagle if we have too many bags attached to our wings—like a bag lady. Remember Erika Badu—bag lady. "You gone hurt yourself dragging all those bags like that." Pack light! Heavy bags cause you to abort! A closed door! Now is the time for confession and self-reflection! Think about the stuff in your bags. I have shared a few examples of my experiences, and some may have felt like punishment (recycle) when those experiences were actually preparation to go to the next level. Sometimes, in the luggage are people y'all. Everybody can't always go to the next level—recognize that. Unpack those things that are weights and create barriers between you and God that can sometimes delay or ultimately deny your blessing. Recently, I read someplace that sometimes you have to move people from the VIP section of your life, and give them seats in general admission.

The Delay

Do you believe that we cause our own delay and/or denial? Could that be from of our inability to demonstrate mastery of the specific knowledge or behavior? God has identified something that has to be purged. Let it go, or learn it! Go get your blessing. Delay has happened to me often enough for me to share how I delayed my own blessings. Remember the ***experience*** that was to help me understand the power of prayer and my gift as an intercessor. I was obviously not praying often enough. That was a three-year class that could have gone a lot faster, had God just told me (IJS). Remember, ***the experience*** I already shared was to teach me to stop fighting people and situations and see that God was a much better fighter than I ever could be. Talk about recycling. That was a ten- to fifteen-year class! Some lessons are harder to learn than others. I just said that, right? It's hard to stop fighting when you had to fight for neighborhood survival though. ***One of my favorite experiences*** was designed to teach me that regardless of how I was being treated, I had to show love. Of course, I still I have to be reminded of this lesson from time to time. I told you that once I mastered the lesson, God came back later and took that lesson and amplified it times ten. He basically said, "When people look at you, they must see God!" Thankfully, I had experienced enough life lessons with God that I was surely ready to be obedient. I want my life to be a source of inspiration and encouragement for my kids. However, that was a tall order. What does people "seeing" God in me mean beyond the many obvious sacrifices? Sometimes, for a diamond to really shine, it must be expertly cut and polished to maximize the diamond's natural brilliance. However, silver requires a purification process. Purify means "to burn away, to cleanse..."

I'm reminded of a story I read several years ago. See below...

The Purification

Words of wisdom; Malachi the, "refiner and purifier of silver." Malachi 3:3 NIV says, "He will sit as a refiner and purifier of silver."

This verse puzzled some women in a Bible study, and they wondered what this statement meant about the character and nature of God. One of the women offered to find out the process of refining silver and get back to the group at their next Bible Study. That week, the woman called a silversmith and made an appointment to watch him at work. She didn't mention anything about the reason for her interest beyond her curiosity about the process of refining silver. As she watched the silversmith, he held a piece of silver over the fire and let it heat up. He explained that in refining silver, one needed to hold the silver in the middle of the fire where the flames were hottest as to burn away all the impurities. The woman thought about God holding us in such a hot spot, then she thought again about the verse that says, "He sits as a refiner and purifier of silver." She asked the silversmith if it was true that he had to sit there in front of the fire the whole time the silver was being refined. The man answered that yes, he not only had to sit there holding the silver, but he had to keep his eyes on the silver the entire time it was in the fire. If the silver was left a moment too long in the flames, it would be destroyed. The woman was silent for a moment. Then she asked the silversmith, "How do you know when the silver is fully refined?" He smiled at her and answered, "Oh, that's easy—when I see my image in it" (www.silversmithing.com). Today, if you are feeling the heat of the fire, remember that God has His eye on you and will keep watching you until He sees His image in you.

Remember, He required that of me a little while ago. I came across this story while facilitating a workshop at my place of employment. As I prepared, God said, "You know I need you to talk about me." I said, "At work, God? I am the head of human resources, how do I do that?" I trusted Him and allowed Him to show me how to do what He asked. What a great day that turned out to be. Under extreme scrutiny and a watchful eye, God still managed to get the glory without me saying His name once. However, I still represented Him and His light shone brightly that day. Also, each of my presenters arrived dressed in black without being asked. Somehow, I knew that was God's message of solidarity, and I knew we were all on one accord that day.

I'm starting to really get excited. Partnering with God as He leads has been an amazing experience. The highs, the lows, the closed doors, the many, many blessings and the opportunities to be a blessing is causing my heart to overflow.

Refocus—your next chapter is beginning to take shape.

However, this race is not given to the swift…

"While the earth remaineth, seedtime and harvest, and
Cold and heat, and summer and winter,
and day and night shall not cease."
—Genesis 8:22

Those who walk with God always reach their destination!

Chapter Eight

Walking with God

It's a Marathon, Not a Sprint

We have been on some journey. I wanted to simply talk about my closed-door experience. God obviously had another plan as usual. So what **time** is this? What's the plan? I still really had no idea. He said, start a business—what does that mean exactly? God is so awesome though. Sometimes He answers prayers even before we ask. While I had more questions than I had answers, God put some amazing people in my path at the right **time** to answer questions and to point me in the right direction. It has been pretty awesome. All because I was open to the possibilities and willing to trust God. Now what's ahead of me is a marathon, not a sprint. As a new business owner, you must do all the work yourself. I was creating an infrastructure for my business, while trying to satisfy all local, state, and federal requirements to become a business owner. To market myself, I also had to simultaneously network and request meetings to introduce myself to some and ensure others knew I was still around. Working for yourself definitely has its privileges. However, the effort is absolutely a different kind of work. You encounter all sorts of people along the way. While some individuals were extremely helpful, others were put in my path to simply be a distraction. The challenge was being able to discern the difference between the two. Some of that I am still trying to figure out. Suffice it to say, some former VIPs now have seats in the cheap section.

I was creating letterhead, marketing materials for my company, and doing research and networking for contract opportunities, all at the same time. When you are self-employed, if you don't work, you don't eat. Now, that's serious motivation. I promised God that I was not going to waste this **time** he had given me. I chose to look at this **time** as a gift from God to allow me to do some of the things I had not had **time** to do previously—like writing a book or two. Every day I did something until I landed my first contract, and I haven't stopped, nor have I looked back (remember, the lights are out anyway). God has a way of motivating us to line up with His plan for our lives. He also figures out the details that can be overwhelming. The key is to listen and be watchful.

Just prior to receiving that first contract, my pay was running out, and I was feeling like Simon Peter in Mark chapter 1—no fish; follow me. I had no other option, so I packed up and followed Jesus. Unlike Peter who had no hesitation or second thought, I did have some doubtful moments like when my paychecks completely stopped. However, like Peter, I kept pressing forward because I know, like I knew my name, that God was in control. I know He had a plan, and I had to trust Him even though I was looking at a closed door. Are you really asking why I keep telling you this? God wants to make sure you get it! I still had to be careful as I did not know what was happening around me or what was next. What was real for me was the fact that I was in preparation mode. I was encountering challenges that could cause me to abort. I had to be watchful. Each **time** I needed a financial blessing, God came through. This journey has not been easy. I would not be being truthful if I told you otherwise. What was for certain for me was God had to have a plan, and I had to trust Him and say yes often during His process.

I'm thankful that I know God. I'm even more thankful that I have learned to trust him. I can't imagine life for an individual experiencing this kind of uncertainty without knowing God. My relationship with God has made this journey less stressful and even enjoyable. He has enabled me to embrace this **time** and to experience him on a level I didn't know was possible.

Because we really don't know what God is doing, it should be a major source of comfort in knowing that God always has his eye on us. We sing a song that says His eye is on the sparrow and I know He watches over me. Do you really believe that He is always watching? Well then, you have to believe that He is always prepared for our unexpected. What is the lesson? Where are you going, and how will you get there? I don't know where God is taking me, but I know He holds the future, so I'm going to walk with Him.

The closed door might end up being a blessing if you believe. So don't be disappointed just yet! God has a plan...

Believing God MEANS trusting Him, EVEN when you don't understand His PLAN.

Faith is trusting God,

Even when you don't understand His Plan!!

Chapter Nine

Believing God!

How many times have we stared at a closed door? That experience causes shock, disbelief, anger, denial, regret, and any other emotion when staring at a door slammed shut. We feel stuck. Sometimes like a child, we have to be dragged away from the closed door, kicking and screaming while peeling our fingers off the doorframe. What a sight! Remember, we agreed that we must **trust** God more so we can **stress** less. Ignoring or denying a closed door is like holding on to rotten fruit that has stayed on the vine too long. It's like a baby not wanting to be born because they were comfortable in the womb, not knowing what's behind the next door. Let's do ourselves a favor and quickly recognize that when God has shut the door or has allowed the door to close, let it go! We have to get ready for the next phase of God's plan to unfold. Remember we have already reflected on previous closed-doors and they have all been for our benefit. The closed door ends a season, not His plan. Time for something better? Remember we have already reflected on previous closed doors. We agreed that all of those closings have been for our good.

Did you ever think the door had to close just so you could do something amazing? When the door closes, trusting His process is the key. I just thought of a couple who was forced to move out of their apartment last year. When I saw the husband, he was angry and seemingly distraught. As he shared his frustration of having to move with no real plan, all I could say was, "trust God." About a year later, I saw the same couple in a home store shopping. With the biggest smile on his face, the formerly angry, agitated husband told me they had just purchased their first house. I said, "Wasn't it just last year that you told me that you were forced to move?" Now here it was, three weeks before Christmas the following year, and they were shopping for items for the new home that they just went to settlement closing the week prior. They had to be pushed to do something that made them extremely uncomfortable, in order for God to bless them. So again, when the door closes, trust God, and say yes to His process. Unlike us, He always has a plan.

Alexander Graham Bell said, "When one door closes, another opens, but we often look so long and so regretfully upon the closed door that we do not see the one which has been opened for us." **Pay attention!** Believe God! We *must* watchfully look for God's next open door. I would hate for you to miss the revelation of the next path. This may be a door of opportunity and not necessarily an actual opened door. We have to be willing to explore every potential opportunity. Knock hard (through challenging work, persistence, and perseverance) until you find the opened door. A door—multiple doors will open. When those doors open depends on you. My mom would say, "You can lead horses to water, but you can't make them drink." We should be working these things while we "wait on the Lord; be of good courage and He shall strengthen your heart; wait I say on the Lord" (Psalm 27:14 KJV). ***Wait*** in service to the Lord, like a servant or a restaurant waiter. We are to continue to serve him while we go through the trying waters of challenging times. Again, to wait does not mean to sit around and do nothing; it means to serve. This is an appropriate time to ask...How may I serve you, Lord? "Ask, and it shall be given to you; seek, and ye shall find; knock, and [the door] shall be opened unto you:" (Matthew 7:7 KJV). Eva Cassidy wrote the song, *"Wade in the Water."* Remember, no matter what Gods gonna trouble the water. Maybe you're the young girl dressed in red that Moses led; or perhaps you're the young girl dressed in white that is an Israelite. Is that you over yonder dressed in blue? Those are the children that are coming through. So just wade in the water, wade in the water children, because God will trouble your waters.

We often miss our blessing to serve when we spend too much **time** either sitting in disbelief, or paralyzed just staring at the closed door. We spend all our **time** trying to reopen the door. Or we overanalyze why the door closed in the first place. Better yet, we waste **time** justifying why we need to find a cracked window or another door to get back in, like an unhealthy relationship! Please believe God and be willing to serve Him with gladness!

During that advent season, God closed a door. No need to look around for assistance because help was not coming. I stopped looking back because not only was the door closed, the lights were already out, and the moving company had already been called. I didn't know where I was going, but it was obviously time to go. While I was absolutely trusting God, it still felt like I was in a boat in the middle of the ocean, and all I could see in front of me was the sea of the abyss. There was nothing but water, and the water was as far as the eye could see. Sometimes our problems have more purpose than we can image. However, I was ready to move and follow God's lead. He told me to trust Him, take His hand, close my eyes, and jump! Like Peter, it was only me and God—in the boat. (Didn't Steve Harvey write a book like that?)

Even though the water looked like it was deep, I trusted God, and I jumped. I thought I could jump close to the boat just in case the water was too deep. However, what I didn't know was, there was a springboard beneath where I was standing. God is so funny that way. When I jumped, somehow, I catapulted, and I was launched into the deep. Years ago, someone told me that I would do just that! Yup, boy o' boy, the water was deep and momentarily over my head. Of course, God would never let me drown. Instead, when I started to tread water and came up for air, God was right there. He immediately showed me what to do. At that time, going back to work full-time was not God's plan. When I tried to pursue money, He sat me down. (I know some of you think that's a bad idea—that's why I trust God—IJS). Godly moves are not for the natural mind to even process. God said, write a book and start a consulting business. Of course, both were foreign to me. But here we are. All I had to do was to be willing to let go! Tell me God is not an awesome God!

Remember that was not my plan! People think I have failed; on the contrary, I've been promoted! My consulting business is doing well, and I work my own schedule. March 2017 was a good **time** to start a business. Not only are my bills paid, but five months later, I was also able to start saving money again. Yes, I had some rough patches, and yes, it has been a financial adjustment. I still consider it a temporary state of being. While depending on man, this would be impossible. However, "but with God all things are possible." (Matthew 19:26 KJV). I'm believing God, and I am standing on that promise. You are now reading man's impossible.

When you find yourself in the middle of a storm, you must prepare yourself for the rain. Be patient and wait in service while the storm passes. Trouble does not last always. Rain clouds do move, and Jesus will always be the sunshine right after the rain. That was a song too, right? If you ask me, it's mighty nice to be on the Lord's side. Remember, in order for the diamond to sparkle and for gold to glow, they must be refined and/or gone through the fire. It's a necessary process. Without the fire, there is no shine; there is no glitter. Are you facing darkness? Has a door closed? Trust God and His process. I've said trust God so much that I hope you got the message. Maybe the door had to close in order to make way for God's plan. How many times have you said…"If it had not been for this [situation], I would have never experienced…" So don't be disappointed when a door closes. As you process through your human emotions, allow God the freedom to show you in His magnificent way that He is still the God of more than enough, and He is there to weather the storm with you! Something great is on its way, and it's just for you! The fact that you are reading my book, a book I would have never written had the door not closed, is proof that God reigns! When you are seemingly down to nothing, God is always up to something!

Rest in the assurance that God has everything in control.

Let us not become weary in doing good, for the proper time we will reap a harvest if we do not give up. Therefore, as we have opportunity, let us do good to all people, especially to those who belong to the family of believers (Galatians 6:9–10, NIV).

Until next time, remember, I am because...

God is my protection. God is my all in all. God is my light in darkness. God is my all in all.

[Verse 2] God is my joy in time of sorrow. God is my all in all. God is my today and tomorrow. God is my all in all.

[Chorus] God is the joy and the strength of my life, He moves all pain, misery, and strife. He promised to keep me, never to leave me. He'll never ever come short of His Word.

I've got to fast and pray, stay in His narrow way, I'll keep my life clean every day; I want to go with Him when He comes back, I've come too far, and I'll never turn back.

God is [3×], God is my all in all.

James Cleveland

CPSIA information can be obtained
at www.ICGtesting.com
Printed in the USA
LVHW020619270620
659109LV00008B/322

9 781098 032043